leap THROUGH

The First Humans

illustrated by
Peter Dennis

BACKPACK BOOKS
NEW YORK

Contents

6 950,000 years ago...
The world is in the grip of the Ice Ages. A cave bear spends the cold winter in a deep sleep.

8 100,000 years later...
Humans have discovered a cave—somewhere to shelter for the night. Suddenly a pack of lions attacks them.

10 350,000 years later...
Prehistoric humans still use the cave for shelter. For food, they hunt wild animals with their wooden spears.

12 400,000 years later...
Neanderthals have set up camp inside the cave mouth. Their clothes are made from animals skins and furs.

14 A few weeks later...
The Neanderthal hunters have trapped a woolly mammoth.

16 The next day...
The Neanderthals prepare to bury a man. His body is laid in a pit along with the skull of a deer.

18 65,000 years later...
The Neanderthals have visitors. They are friendly, although the Neanderthals cannot understand what they are saying.

20 10,000 years later...
Modern humans have taken over the cave. Some are at work painting pictures of animals on the cave walls.

22 20,000 years later...
No one lives in the cave. People still hunt and fish, but they have now also become farmers.

24 A few years ago...
A school party visits the cave. Some children manage to squeeze through the narrow opening. An astonishing sight greets them.

26 A few months later...
Archaeologists are carrying out a very detailed excavation. Soon they make an exciting discovery.

28 Today
The cave, with its magnificent paintings discovered by the schoolchildren, is now a tourist attraction.

30 Glossary

31 Index

Introduction

Imagine you are somewhere in Europe, at the entrance to a cave on the slopes of a mountain valley. It is hundreds of thousands of years ago. Some humans use the cave as a shelter. They wear no clothes, their bodies are covered with hair, and the shape of their heads is different from ours. As thousands of years pass, gradually the humans evolve and change. They become expert hunters and toolmakers and learn to make clothes. Then they die out and modern humans arrive to take over the cave.

The story told in this book is like a journey. It is not a journey you can make by plane, car, or ship. In fact, you don't have to go anywhere at all. You are about to travel through *time*. With each turn of the page, the date moves forward many thousands of years—or sometimes just a short period. Each stop on the journey is like a chapter in the story. The first settlers, the encounters with wild animals, the capture of a woolly mammoth, the burial of the dead hunter, the cave paintings—all tell the story of the first humans.

Look out for a pair of bats. They appear in all of the illustrations, although sometimes they are quite difficult to spot.

Use this thumb index to travel through time! Just find the page you want to see and flip it open. This way you can make a quick comparison between one scene and another, even though some show events that took place many years apart. A little black arrow on the page points to the time of the scene illustrated on that page.

950,000 years ago...

The world is in the grip of the Ice Ages. In Europe, summers are short and cool, while winters are long and severe. Watched by a big cat, a herd of wild horses is under attack by a pack of hyenas. Meanwhile, in a nearby cave, a cave bear spends the cold winter in a deep sleep.

OUT OF AFRICA

Humans first evolved from apes in Africa. No one knows exactly how long ago. Early kinds of hominids (humanlike beings) are known as *Australopithecus*. The first hominids to leave Africa reached Central Asia about 1.8 million years ago.

950,000 years ago

Wild sheep

Cave bear asleep in cave

Horses

Wolves

Big cat

Humans share a common ancestor with the apes.

100,000 years later . . .

Humans (not quite like present-day people) have arrived in the valley. They have discovered a cave—somewhere to shelter for the night. Suddenly a pack of lions attacks them. The humans defend themselves with spears. But their most powerful weapon is fire. Some of them have brought burning brands from a bushfire. They pass the fire around to all the others. The lions pull back in alarm. Eventually they skulk away. The humans make their shelter comfortable. They will travel on in the morning.

950,000 years ago

850,000 years ago

Unlike other apes, humans walk upright on two legs. This feature allows humans to carry things, make tools, and do things with our hands.

350,000 years later . . .

Prehistoric humans still use the cave for shelter. For food, they hunt wild animals with their wooden spears. They use stone tools to scrape flesh from the bones. They cook the meat over a fire and eat it with their fingers. Suddenly there is a roar. A fierce bear has appeared on the opposite bank of the stream. They scare it away by throwing spears and stones at it.

Bear

Berries

Making stone tools

For these people, wild animals are still a threat. But they have become skilled at defending themselves.

BIG BRAINS

By 500,000 years ago, *Homo heidelbergensis* (known as "heidelbergs") had evolved in Europe. These new kinds of humans had much more brainpower than their ancestors. As well as gathering fruits and nuts to eat, heidelbergs hunted large animals, tracking them and ambushing them with stealth and cunning. They worked together as a team, and were probably able to talk—although not in quite the same way that modern humans do. They used stone tools to cut up the carcasses of the animals they had killed. With their carefully crafted spears and superior intelligence, heidelbergs were expert hunters.

Making spears

Cooking over fire

950,000 years ago

850,000 years ago

500,000 years ago

The 3.2-million-year-old skeleton of *Australopithecus afarensis*, known as "Lucy," was discovered in 1974.

400,000 years later . . .

Once more, the cave has new residents. The Neanderthal people who live there are different from their ancestors—but not the same as modern people.

The climate is gradually turning colder. The Neanderthals have set up camp inside the cave mouth. Their clothes are made from animal skins and furs. They cook fish and meat over fires. Tusks and skins are used in the building of shelters.

Visiting group

Shelter made from animal skins

Skins

Making spears

The men show the children how to make fire and to craft blades from stone. A baby is born deep inside the cave, where it is warmer and drier.

THE NEANDERTHALS

From about 400,000 years ago, *Homo heidelbergensis* evolved into a new kind of human, *Homo neanderthalensis* (or Neanderthal). It was named after the German valley where the first fossil bones were discovered in 1856. At first, the bones were thought to belong to a horseman injured in battle with Napoleon's armies. Scientists later realized it was a prehistoric human. Neanderthals had short, muscular bodies. Their heads had low foreheads, thick brow ridges, and wide noses. Their brains were, on average, larger than those of modern humans.

Newborn baby

Inner cave

Entrance to inner cave

Making fire

Spearhead

Treating injury

950,000 years ago

850,000 years ago

500,000 years ago

100,000 years ago

A few weeks later . . .

The Neanderthal hunters have trapped a woolly mammoth. They dug a pit and waited for a herd to approach. Then they rushed at the giant animals with flaming torches, driving one of them into the trap.

Cave

Hunter tossed to the ground

Fossilized footprints in volcanic sediments were discovered at Laetoli, East Africa, in 1976. They were made 3.6 million years ago by apemen, probably *Australopithecus afarensis*, no more than 5 feet tall.

The mammoth writhes and roars in a desperate attempt to climb out of the pit, but to no avail. The hunters move in for the kill. They thrust their long, heavy spears into its sides. At that moment, the mammoth suddenly rears up. Using its mighty, curved tusks, it hoists one of the hunters into the air. The man is tossed to the ground where he lands with a sickening thud. He is fatally wounded.

950,000 years ago

850,000 years ago

500,000 years ago

100,000 years ago

A few weeks later

Homo habilis, whose name means "handy man," probably evolved from a kind of *Australopithecus* about 2.5 million years ago in Africa. It may have been the first hominid capable of making simple stone tools.

The next day . . .

The hunters succeeded in bringing down their prey. The meat, fur, tusks, and bones will all be used by the group. But the success came at dreadful cost.

The wounded hunter died of his injuries soon afterward. The others carried him back to the cave, full of sadness. Other members of the group gathered around. They remembered so many men who had suffered injuries while hunting. Some they had been able to care for until the injuries healed. Others, like this man,

Cooking over fire

Dropped arrowhead

Spearhead

died. No one in the group has lived to older than 45 years.

Now the Neanderthals prepare to bury the man. They dig a pit. His body is laid in it, along with the skin of a wolf and the skull of a deer. A woman and her children sprinkle flower petals into the grave.

Burial ceremony

950,000 years ago

850,000 years ago

500,000 years ago

100,000 years ago

A few weeks later

The next day

Homo ergaster evolved in Africa about 2 million years ago. Descendants of this kind of human, tall and powerfully built, traveled to other continents. They probably went in search of new hunting grounds, as meat had become an important part of their diet. Bones of their descendants, *Homo erectus*, have been found in Java, China, and Central Asia.

65,000 years later . . .

The Neanderthals huddle together for warmth inside the cave. They have barely enough food to last the winter. The herds that once came to the valley no longer appear.

Just then, they hear footsteps. The Neanderthals greet their visitors with suspicion. They notice right away that they are not like them. (They are, in fact, modern humans—like us.)

The visitors are friendly, although the Neanderthals cannot understand what

Visiting modern humans

they are saying. The visitors carry better weapons than they do. Their clothes are more finely made. They wear ornaments that the Neanderthals love to feel. These people seem to come from another world.

MODERN HUMANS

Like *Homo ergaster* nearly 2 million years before them, *Homo sapiens*—modern humans—originated in Africa and traveled from there to other parts of the world. They arrived in Europe about 40,000 years ago. Within 10,000 years, all the Neanderthals had died out, maybe because modern humans were better able to find food and shelter than they were.

Inner cave

950,000 years ago

850,000 years ago

500,000 years ago

100,000 years ago

A few weeks later

The next day

35,000 years ago

Homo heidelbergensis had emerged by about 500,000 years ago. These humans were forced to learn how to survive a period of rapid climate change. They used their brains to invent better tools. The hammer head *(top)* was carved from the antler of a giant deer. Clearly a treasured possession, it was used to make hand axes *(above)* from flints.

10,000 years later . . .

Modern humans have taken over the cave. From the depths come drumming, dancing, clapping, and chanting. Through the dim light given off by the flickering lamps and fire brands, we can just see a group of people. Some are dressed up as animals and perform a dance to the music of a flute player and drummer.

950,000 years ago

850,000 years ago

500,000 years ago

100,000 years ago

A few weeks later

The next day

35,000 years ago

25,000 years ago

Meanwhile, other people are at work painting pictures of animals on the cave walls. Using both tools and their own fingers, they paint with charcoal and ocher, a type of clay.

CAVE PAINTINGS

Some of the most revealing things left behind by our early *Homo sapiens* ancestors were cave paintings. They have been found all over the world. Paintings found at Chauvet, France, date back about 32,000 years ago. It is thought that special ceremonies may have been held in the painted caves.

20,000 years later . . .

No one lives in the cave. People still hunt and fish, but they have now also become farmers. They grow wheat and barley and raise cattle and pigs. They have built shelters from mud, branches, and straw and live together in villages.

A site that has provided a great deal of evidence about early humans is La Sima de los Huesos (the Pit of Bones) in northern Spain. Here the remains of at least 32 humans, dating to 400,000 years ago, have been found at the bottom of a 50-foot shaft. The humans may have been ancestors of the Neanderthals. It is possible that their dead bodies may have been thrown into the pit by their relatives.

THE FIRST FARMERS

For thousands of years modern humans lived by hunting animals, fishing, and gathering fruit, nuts, roots, and honey. They traveled from place to place, following the animals they hunted. They tamed wolves, which became the first hunting dogs.

Once people discovered how to grow the plants they needed rather than go looking for them, they no longer had to travel around to find food, but could settle in the same place and become farmers.

950,000 years ago

850,000 years ago

500,000 years ago

100,000 years ago

A few weeks later

The next day

35,000 years ago

25,000 years ago

5,000 years ago

A few years ago...

A school party visits the valley. The teachers want to show the children the cave. Important finds of old stone tools

The Neanderthals made many cleverly designed tools. These blades, chipped from flakes of rock, were made so that they fit snugly into the hand. Teeth from moose and wolves were worn as pendants.

The Neanderthals lived hard, dangerous lives. Many of their bones that have been discovered (such as this rib bone) show evidence of serious injury. The crippled members of the group were fed and cared for by the others.

in recent years suggest that prehistoric people once lived there. If all the children search carefully, they may even discover more exciting finds, such as a spearhead or even ancient bones!

In the last few days, a pile of rubble that was blocking the entrance to the inner cave has fallen away. No one knew that the cave was, in fact, much deeper. Now some children manage to squeeze through the narrow opening. Some of them shine flashlights and an astonishing sight greets them. On the walls are some paintings of animals, not seen by anyone else for many thousands of years.

Entrance to inner cave

Cave paintings

950,000 years ago

850,000 years ago

500,000 years ago

100,000 years ago

A few weeks later

The next day

35,000 years ago

25,000 years ago

5,000 years ago

A few years ago

Homo sapiens—modern humans—probably first emerged in Africa around 200,000 years ago. About 100,000 years ago, they began to spread around the globe. They reached Indonesia and Australia 60,000 years ago. By 40,000 years ago they had arrived in Europe.

Humans arrived in North America between 35,000 and 15,000 years ago. They crossed from Asia at a time when the Bering Sea, which divides the two continents, was dry land. They then spread through the Americas, reaching the southern tip of South America 11,000 years ago.

A few months later . . .

The children returned to their school very excited about what they had found. Their teacher contacted an expert at the local museum. Soon, a team of archaeologists specializing in early humans visited the cave. They quickly realized that the children had made an extremely important discovery.

Now the archaeologists are carrying out a very detailed excavation. In the inner cave, a grid has been set up, dividing the cave floor into squares. This allows them to record precisely where any finds have been discovered. They

Drawing of mammoth

Entrance to inner cave

Sieving

Discovery of burial

carefully brush away layers of soil in their search for tools, weapons, or even bones or teeth.

In the cave mouth, the team dig a trench, to see what might lie just below the surface. Soon they make another very exciting discovery. They find the pit where the Neanderthal hunter was buried *(see page 17)*. His bones have lain undisturbed for 100,000 years.

Cave paintings

Archaeological excavation

Grid

Hearth

Finds

950,000 years ago

850,000 years ago

500,000 years ago

100,000 years ago

A few weeks later

The next day

35,000 years ago

25,000 years ago

5,000 years ago

A few years ago

A few months later

Discoveries of bones, tools and weapons in Africa all provide evidence that modern humans emerged in that continent. This carved bone harpoon *(above)*, found in Africa, is about 90,000 years old.

By about 35,000 years ago, modern humans were expressing themselves in producing art forms. This tiny sculpture of a woman's head *(above)*, known as the Lady of Brassempouy, was carved from mammoth ivory about 25,000 years ago. Ornaments may have been worn by important members of a community.

Today

The cave, with its magnificent paintings discovered by the schoolchildren, is now a tourist attraction. Near the entrance to the cave a man dressed as a Neanderthal gives a demonstration of how his people used stone flakes as tools. Close by, actors re-create the burial of the hunter.

A narrow entrance leads to the inner cave. Models show how the Neanderthals cooked food over a fire. Another shows how the cave's first resident, a bear, might have chased away a human invader!

The cave paintings are on display. They astonish all who see them. They have been encased in glass to protect them from the changing temperature and from moisture in the air. The visitors try to imagine how and when they were painted. You need only look back to page 20 to find out for yourself!

950,000 years ago

850,000 years ago

500,000 years ago

100,000 years ago

A few weeks later

The next day

35,000 years ago

25,000 years ago

5,000 years ago

A few years ago

A few months later

Today

Glossary

Archaeologist A person who studies past human life and culture, using the evidence from finds buried in the ground or under the sea.

Australopithecus An apelike hominid. *Australopithecus* lived in Africa between 4 and 2 million years ago. Fossils of several kinds, including *afarensis, anamensis, africanus,* and *garhi,* have been discovered. Some may have been ancestors of humans.

Climate change In every region of the world, there is a regular pattern of weather over a period of time—rain, wind, temperature, etc. This pattern is called a climate. A region's climate may change over time. This may be for a number of reasons, including variations in the sun's heat or the gradual movement of the continents around the globe over millions of years.

Evolution The process by which forms of life have changed over millions of years, gradually adapting to make best use of their environment.

Excavation Digging out and removing fossils, bones, or manmade objects from the ground.

Flint A hard sedimentary rock, composed chiefly of quartz. Flints are found in limestone and chalk. Flint may be chipped to form a sharp cutting edge and was used by prehistoric humans to make tools.

Fossils The ancient remains or traces of once-living things, usually found preserved in rock. A living thing becomes fossilized when it is buried by sediments and its hard parts are gradually replaced by minerals.

Hand ax A piece of stone, shaped like a teardrop, used by prehistoric humans as a knife to cut meat.

Heidelberg A short name for *Homo heidelbergensis,* an extinct hominid that evolved in Europe and was the ancestor of the Neanderthals.

Hominid A human or human relative, including all prehistoric kinds. The word is usually used to describe early humans and their relatives, for example, *Australopithecus* or *Homo erectus.*

Homo erectus An extinct hominid, descended from *Homo ergaster,* that lived in Asia.

Homo ergaster An extinct hominid that emerged in Africa about 2 million years ago. It was the first hominid to travel out of Africa.

Homo sapiens The species name for modern humans, who first emerged in Africa about 2 million years ago and later spread out to the rest of the world.

Ice Ages A pattern of climate change that began 2.7 million years ago. During the Ice Ages warm and cold periods alternate, each lasting several thousand years. The Ice Ages have not yet come to an end—we are currently living in a warm phase.

Mammoth A type of elephant, now extinct, that lived in Europe from about 2.6 million to 10,000 years ago. Woolly mammoths had hairy coats and long, curved tusks, and lived in cold lands.

Neanderthal A kind of hominid, now extinct, that lived in Europe and the Middle East from about 400,000 to 30,000 years ago.